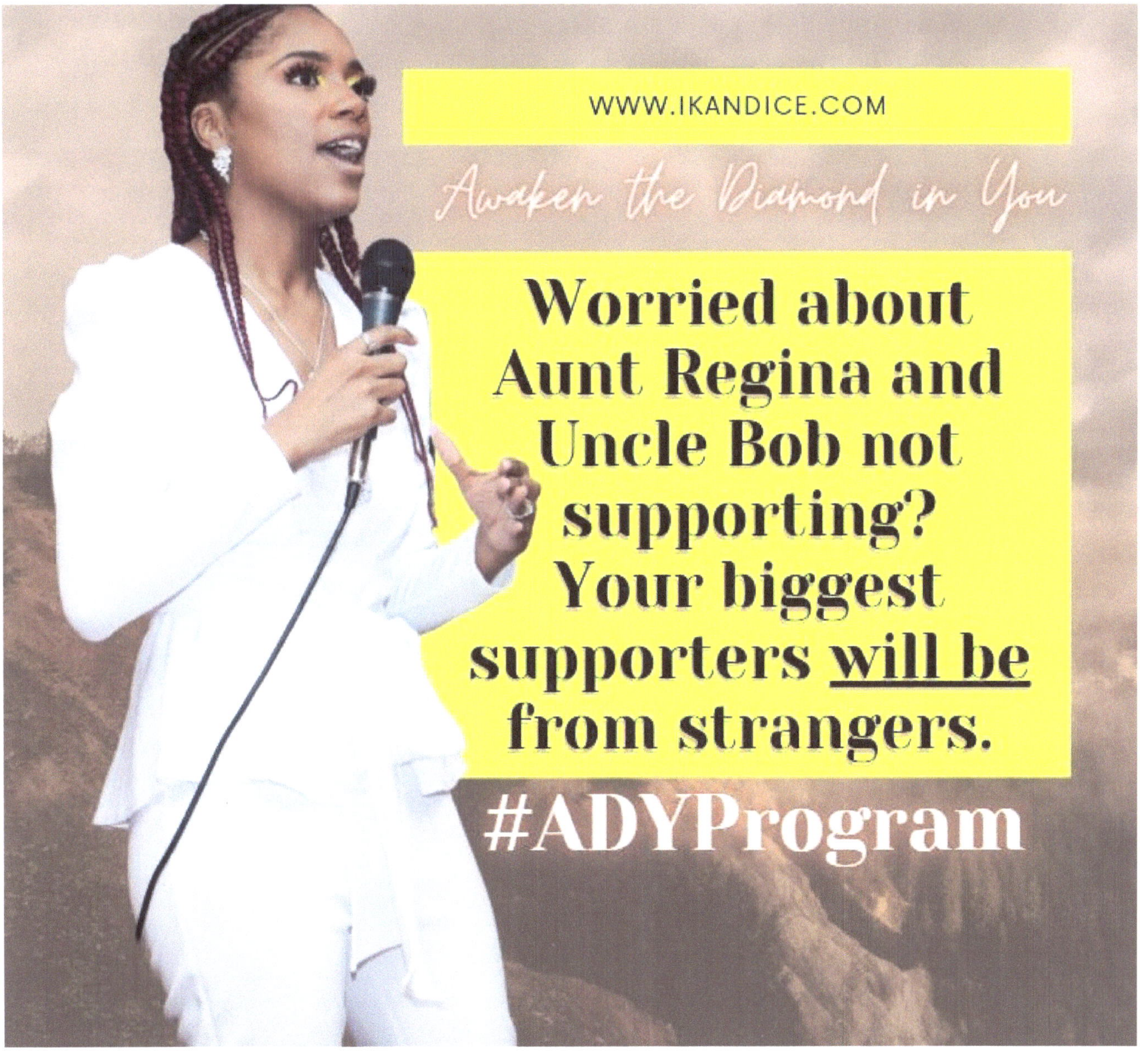

WWW.IKANDICE.COM
Awaken the Diamond in You
Worried about Aunt Regina and Uncle Bob not supporting? Your biggest supporters will be from strangers.
#ADYProgram

Norma's Bath & Body

-Founded in 2004-
Luscious and Addictive Bath and Body.
Ships all across the USA.
Bath and Body that does the body good!
It's the Body Bakery.

NORMASBATHANDBODY.ARTFIRE.COM

Welcomes Bulk Wholesale Orders!

2Pickle'd is based in Waco, TX and we specialize in the best gourmet flavored pickles around. Our product is truly like no other and we invite you to try it for yourself! We received the seal of approval from the big boss himself - Master P. (See below)

www.2Pickled.com | 214-893-2475

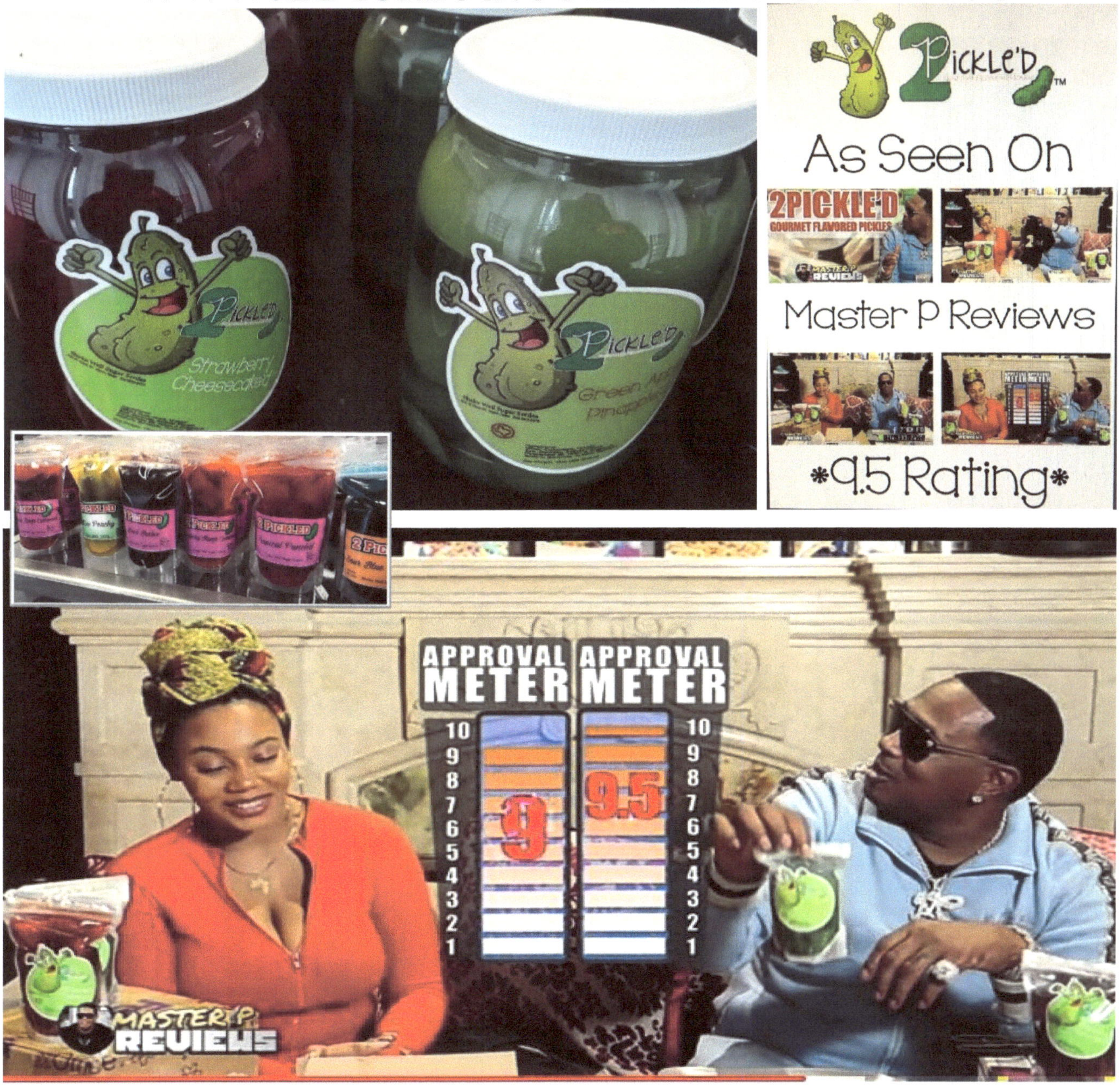

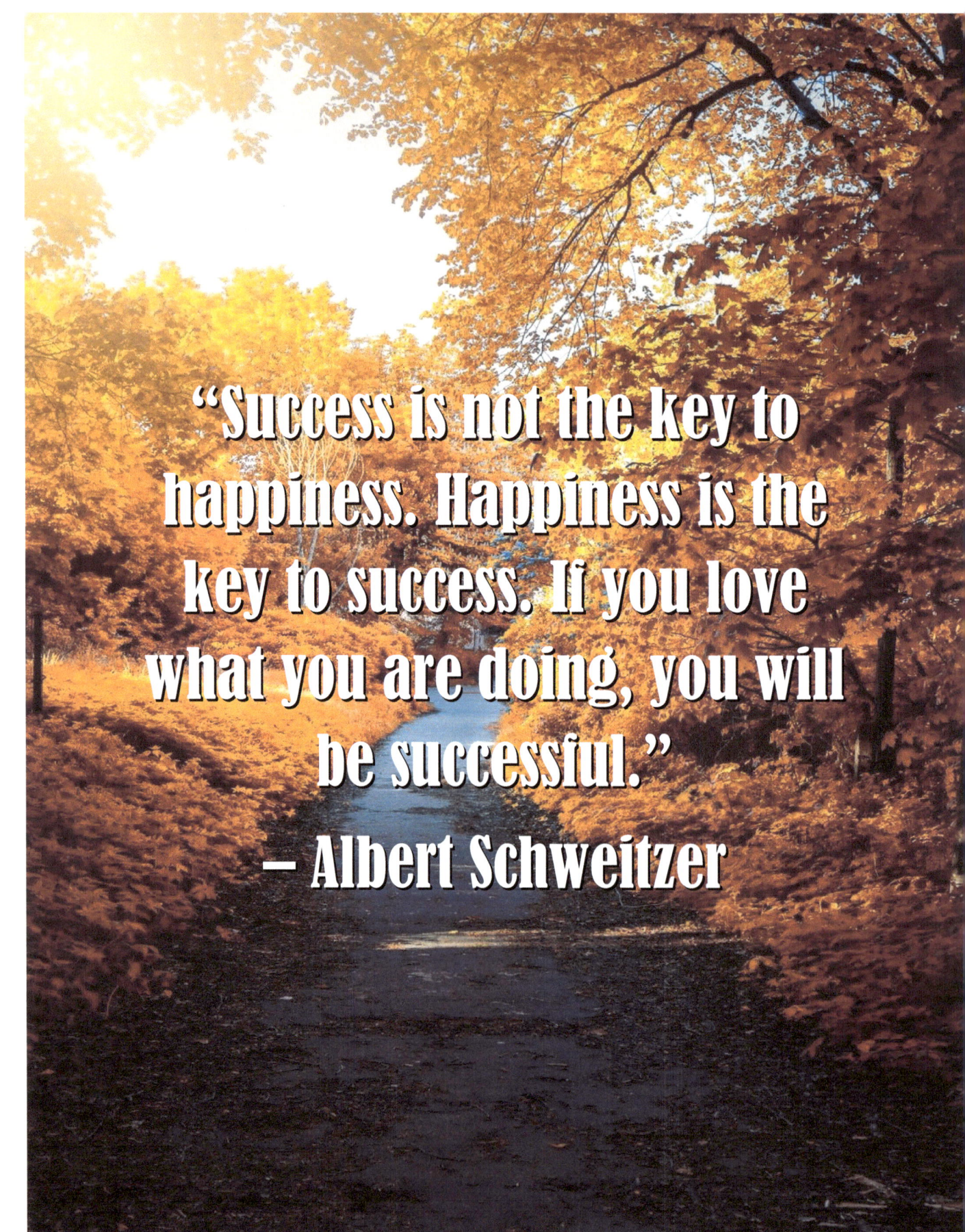

Mattress the Story Holder
lulu.com/spotlight/medwards1

INTERNATIONAL SELLER!

Safety

Tactical Education & Defense, LLC is based in Tampa, FL, but serves the entirety of the state. Our overall goal is to empower responsible citizens to secure their freedom of peace of mind and their Second Amendment rights. This first goal is achieved primarily through education because any tool is useless without the proper knowledge and understanding of its functions. This concept extends to tools of avoidance, the ability to evade, and when to defend. Critical thinking and situational awareness can save lives without anyone having to be involved in an unwarranted scenario. We want to encourage developing the right attitude and thinking things through. Secondly, the defensive component comes from your RIGHT to defend yourself and your family to sustain life. This second goal is accomplished through a holistic approach that integrates education and defense fundamentals into your everyday life.

Not only will you learn this lifestyle, but you will also become the epitome of what it means to be tactically educated with the competence and skills to defend yourself AND your freedom.

We offer individual, family, and group courses that accommodate those who have never held a firearm, seeking home defense fundamentals, firearm safety, purchasing, proficiency, and classes for Florida Concealed Carry Weapons License. The type of courses regarding firearms includes Pistol, Rifle, and Shotgun. You can expect to get more than the minimum as we strive to create a community that raises the standard of what it means to be situationally aware. We are available and flexible to your needs and goals, as this is achieved by providing classes to the surrounding areas, zoom, and traveling to you. Ultimately, we want to make it easier for you to get educated, protect yourself, and gain peace of mind because you are prepared.

**Control the Controllable:
YOUR - Attitude, YOUR - Knowledge, and YOUR - Skills**

When asked about the new gun law in Texas that was passed and set into effect September 1st, 2021, Capers responded,

" As an Instructor, my advice to any Gun owner: I advocate for responsible gun ownership and I strongly encouragecontinuous training on Situational Awareness, Local Firearm Laws, Firearm Safety, and Functionality."

#FreedomSecured

https://linktr.ee/tacticaleducationdefensellc

The Perfect Gifts for the Upcoming Holidays!

www.DestineesFashion.com

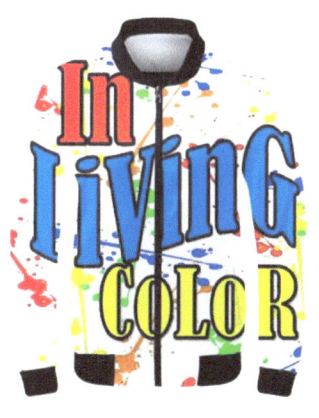

thekandyshop.kincustom.com

11 | DIAMOND ELITE MAGAZINE

Peace comes with rain.

www.PazfulRayn.com

"Who says 33 is too late to start your company?" says Melissa Turner, owner of Pazful Rayn that was launched on March 23, 2021. Turner took the best parts of herself and fused them together by being a mother and being creative.

Pazful Rayn (pronounced Peaceful Rain) was built to remind us that we don't have to wait for the sun to come out to dance. "We can dance in our rain because Peace Comes with Rain. The birth of this legacy is rooted in my love for my two angels. My beautiful 15-year-old daughter, Nevaeh who battles and defeats Autism daily with a smile and my son, Nazir who was granted his wings to be our angel at birth," Turner revealed, "being a parent is a roller coaster ride filled with highs and lows. However, being a single parent of a child with a disability is honestly a whole different level of a roller coaster ride."

Turner stated that it is her daughter's smile that reminds her of why there is always light in a storm, so why wait to dance?

Melissa's Shoutouts: To my daughter Nevaeh, my parents Kathy & Darrell Taylor, and my big sister Amber Wiggins.

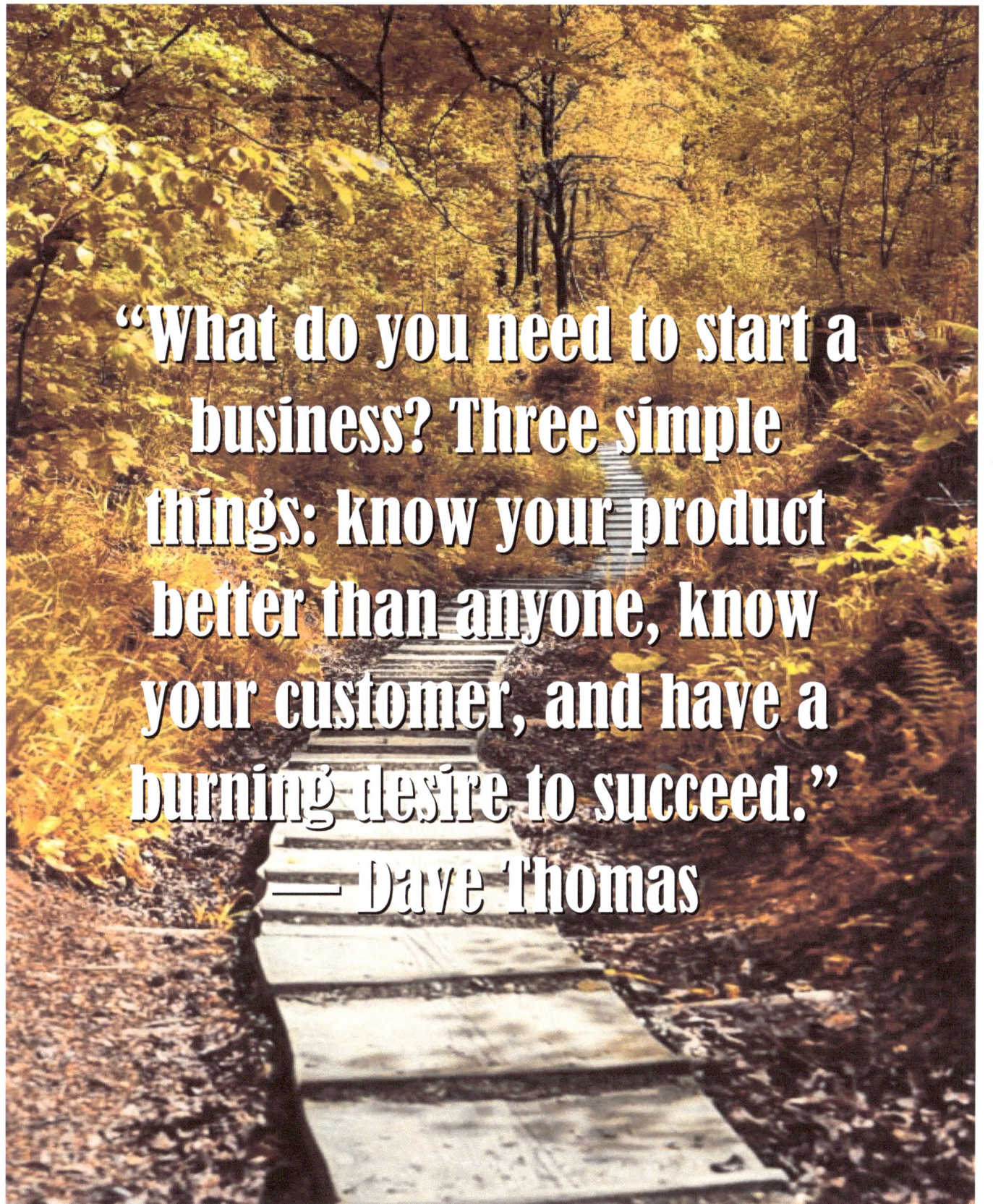

Fall Recipes
Pumpkin Gingerbread

3 cups sugar
1 cup vegetable oil
4 eggs
⅔ cup water
1 (15 ounce) can pumpkin puree
2 teaspoons ground ginger
1 teaspoon ground allspice
1 teaspoon ground cinnamon
1 teaspoon ground cloves
3 ½ cups all-purpose flour
2 teaspoons baking soda
1 ½ teaspoons salt
½ teaspoon baking powder

Directions

- Step 1

Preheat oven to 350 degrees F (175 degrees C). Lightly grease two 9x5 inch loaf pans.

- Step 2

In a large mixing, combine sugar, oil and eggs; beat until smooth. Add water and beat until well blended. Stir in pumpkin, ginger, allspice cinnamon, and clove.

- Step 3

In medium bowl, combine flour, soda, salt, and baking powder. Add dry ingredients to pumpkin mixture and blend just until all ingredients are mixed. Divide batter between prepared pans.

- Step 4

Bake in preheated oven until toothpick comes out clean, about 1 hour.

Prep: 15 mins
Cook: 45 mins
Total: 60 mins
Servings: 24
Yield: 2 - 9x5 inch loaves

Beef Stew

2 pounds cubed beef stew meat
3 tablespoons vegetable oil
4 cubes beef bouillon, crumbled
4 cups water
1 teaspoon dried rosemary
1 teaspoon dried parsley
½ teaspoon ground black pepper
3 large potatoes, peeled and cubed
4 carrots, cut into 1 inch pieces
4 stalks celery, cut into 1 inch pieces
1 large onion, chopped
2 teaspoons cornstarch
2 teaspoons cold water

Directions

- Step 1
  In a large pot or dutch oven, cook beef in oil over medium heat until brown. Dissolve bouillon in water and pour into pot. Stir in rosemary, parsley and pepper. Bring to a boil, then reduce heat, cover and simmer 1 hour.

- Step 2
  Stir potatoes, carrots, celery, and onion into the pot. Dissolve cornstarch in 2 teaspoons cold water and stir into stew. Cover and simmer 1 hour more.

Per Serving: 401 calories; protein 27.2g; carbohydrates 24.9g; fat 21.2g; cholesterol 79mg; sodium 436.3mg

Entertainment

Meet the upcoming artist *CejotaOfficial*, who is now being promoted by Fierce Manson, the founder of The Fierce Female Network, and Abundant Waters Management, Inc.

Cejota was raised in Lynn, MA. CejotaOfficial creates very original music. He is driven and compelled to make music to motivate, inspire, and spread positivity and love to his audience. He also makes music because he is a multi-talented artist that loves the art of sound and is able to construct quality songs. His talent is raw and genuine. He tells his story through his music and is relatable in ways other artists are not. CejotaOfficial stands out musically and is destined to change the game and make a difference in the world.

"We've been formed since July 2021, and to be honest it was just a group of friends with different talents that formed something productive," Cejota shared after being asked how long the group had been in the industry.

His style is versatile and unique. He is working hard by pushing the boundaries set in the music industry to set a name for himself. He demonstrates sound that connects one's mind and body with a positive reaction. CejotaOfficial recently released his EP "CejotaOfficial Presents: tráelo de vuelta" with his lead single "Wine for Me." His music is already making an impact.

When it comes to inspiration, Cejota stated that, " the biggest inspiration would be each other…we go off of everyone's vibe and energy to give each other that push.

CejotaOfficial is becoming the artist and man that he has dreamed of and is inspiring to those around him. On October 2nd CejotaOfficial will be performing their new hit single "Wine for Me" at the BET HIP-HOP Awards Pre-Show.

📷 callmecejota

Advice for Upcoming Artists

"… don't ever get too comfortable and don't ever forget how you started because that rush and beginning of starting something new is refreshing so always work like you never have it." - Cejota

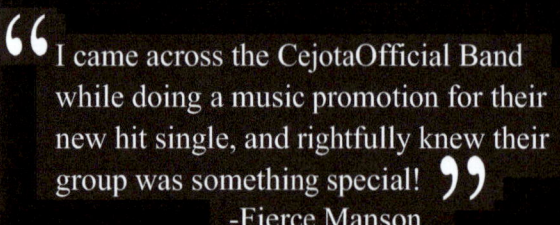

" I came across the CejotaOfficial Band while doing a music promotion for their new hit single, and rightfully knew their group was something special!
-Fierce Manson

Fierce Manson
🐦 thefiercefemale
f thefiercefemale

Ask Genevieve

Genevieve is here to answer any question you may be having an issue with anonymously. Names are not mentioned, just questions and answers.

Question:

Hi, what should I do if my partner isn't supporting my business, or even encouraging me for the least bit?

Answer:

Talk with your partner about this makes you feel. You are not alone when it comes to this topic. The primary barrier with this issue is the lack of communication.

Question:

How do you get the money to even start a business?

Answer:

I would recommend to start saving your personal funds and self-fund your business before going to get a personal loan, although it really depends on your financial stability right now. Pay attention to your debt-to-income ratio.

Question:

How do I know which business to start?

Answer:

If you're not sure which business to start, you may not be an entrepreneur. However, it doesn't hurt to begin with something that you actually like or love doing. If you love writing, start a blog or write a book. If you love sewing, begin offering the service to others that may need items altered, etc. Good luck!

Check Out these Online Stores!

www.phyllisonlinebeautyshop.com

At Phyllis' Store we sell 100% Quality, and standard human hair. We are dedicated to making quality hair available at your disposal, any where any time.

---

ecom-beauty-supply-14504.myshopify.com/

Eyelashes   Face   Haircare   Lips

7 Side Ideas to Begin : Bring in Extra Funds for Your Main Business!

1. Dropshipping – Starting an ecommerce business.
   a. Use eBay, Amazon, etc.
2. Start a Podcast
3. Become a Vlogger
4. Sign up for Rebate Apps
5. Try Out DoorDash, Uber Eats
6. Get good at TikTok and earn money!
7. Grow your followers and engagement on Facebook, you can earn money just by people loving your content and sending "stars" which equal "money!"

> Finance went from being a small business, effectively, to being a big business. In part, that's the growth of the world's wealth. That's called savings.
>
> Jamie Dimon

GOOD NEWS!

The Diamond Elite Magazine Podcast will be returning in 2022!

Discussions will Include:
- ❖ Business (of course)
- ❖ Residual Income
- ❖ Fact or Fiction
- ❖ Strategies
- ❖ Product Reviews
- ❖ and More!

Advertise With Us

Head Over to

www.DiamondEliteMagazine.com

Hit the "Advertise" Tab &
Secure Your Spot for the Q1 2022 Issue!
Ad Slots are *First Come First Serve!*

DIAMOND ELITE
Magazine & Co.